1/18

TRANSGENDER PIONEERS

LAVERNE COX

ROSEN
PUBLISHING

New York

ERIN
STALEY

Published in 2017 by The Rosen Publishing Group, Inc.
29 East 21st Street, New York, NY 10010

Library of Congress Cataloging-in-Publication Data

Names: Staley, Erin, author.
Title: Laverne Cox / Erin Staley.
Description: New York : Rosen Publishing, 2017. | Series: Transgender pioneers | Includes bibliographical references and index.
Identifiers: LCCN 2015047625 | ISBN 9781508171591 (library bound)
Subjects: LCSH: Cox, Laverne. | Transsexuals—United States—Biography. |
  Transgender people—United States—Biography.
Classification: LCC HQ77.8.C69 S73 2017 | DDC 306.76/8092—dc23
LC record available at http://lccn.loc.gov/2015047625

Manufactured in China

CONTENTS

Laverne Cox appears at HBO's Post 2016 Golden Globe Awards Party on January 10, 2016, in Los Angeles, California.

Until recent years, society had largely overlooked transgender rights, leaving the trans community without visibility, equal access to resources, or a platform to promote positive role models. Many have also misunderstood what it means to be transgender, and some have even discriminated against members of the transgender community. Reports of harassment and violence were upsettingly common, and suicide and unemployment rates, disproportionately high.

However, rising above such obstacles, some activists have worked for justice and to end transphobic discrimination. Celebrities in particular have often lent their voices to the trans rights movement in order to bring greater awareness to issues that affect the transgender community at large. These activists share their own experience of identifying as transgender and discuss hurdles they've overcome. In doing so, they give hope to other transgender and gender non-conforming individuals, and they help cisgender individuals gain an understanding of what it means to be transgender. Laverne Cox is one such celebrity activist.

Award-winning actor, advocate, public speaker, dancer, writer, and producer, Laverne Cox is a force both on stage and off. She is intelligent, beautiful, well spoken, and sophisticated, and her presence electrifies the stage in theater productions, television programs, and films. While she has had a number of acting roles, she is best known for playing the role of Sophia Burset on the critically acclaimed Netflix original series *Orange Is the New Black.*

As a transgender pioneer, Cox has enjoyed many firsts. She was the first openly transgender actor to be nominated for a Primetime Emmy and the first openly transgender person to be featured on the cover of *Time* magazine. Cox was the first African American trans woman to participate on a reality competition show (*I Want to Work for Diddy*, 2008), and she was the first transgender woman of color to produce and star in her own television show (*TRANSform Me*, 2010). Cox is even the first transgender person to have a figure modeled after her at Madame Tussauds Wax Museum.

Laverne Cox came from humble beginnings in Mobile, Alabama. She overcame bullying and gender policing as a child, always earning academic achievements and having the courage to be herself. Her tenacity helped her reach her dream of becoming an actor in New York City. Today, her life stands as an example of perseverance, inspiring the transgender community to overcome and to reach for their own dreams.

Cox's success as an entertainer has given her a platform on which to promote awareness of issues that affect the transgender community. She understands that many of the problems faced by her community today are rooted in a lack of public understanding of what it means to be transgender and the legal and social challenges that transgender individuals face. Cox publicly embraces her trans identity, sharing her own personal story in interviews, on talk shows, and at speaking engagements. In doing so, she draws attention to the staggering statistics of discrimination and violence against the transgender community, and promotes open conversations that encourage love and empathy. Laverne Cox is a role model—or in her own words, a "possibility model"—for transgender, gender non-conforming, and cisgender individuals around the world.

CHAPTER 1

MEET LAVERNE COX

Laverne Cox, the Emmy-nominated actor of *Orange Is the New Black* and one of *Time* magazine's "100 Most Influential People" of 2015, has long been an advocate for the transgender community. She has helped countless trans individuals feel connected through her acting roles, university speaking tours, and television guest appearances. However, Cox's life hasn't always been glitz and glamour. She has overcome bullying, gender policing, and even a failed suicide attempt. She's battled discrimination, uncertainty, shame, and conflict—all in a quest to show the world who she is on the inside.

MEET LAVERNE

Laverne Cox and her identical twin brother, Reginald, were born on May 29 in Mobile, Alabama. The twins' birth year is not publicized, although some sources claim that it is 1984. Both twins were assigned male at birth and given names typically associated with men. However, Cox does not publicize the name that she was given at birth. (This decision reflects a common tendency among many members of the transgender community who no longer use the name they were given at birth.) Cox's close friends or family respect her privacy and do not publicize her birth name. However, the actor has acknowledged that Laverne and Cox were her middle and last name, respectively, at the time of her birth.

Laverne and Reginald were raised by their hard-working, church-going single mother, Gloria Cox. Their father was not involved with the family. In a June 2014 article for the Alabama-based news website AL.com, Gloria shared, "I always worked and most of the time had a second job. There was never anything the Lord didn't provide. I did the best I could, and things worked out."

Education and religion were important in the Cox home. Laverne and her brother

Laverne Cox and her mother, Gloria, stand on stage together at the 25th Annual GLAAD Media Awards on April 12, 2014, in Beverly Hills, California.

attended Council Traditional School and Wood-cock Elementary School, and the family was active in the Bethel African Methodist Episcopal Church. Laverne and Reginald were expected by their mother and community to become upstanding, responsible citizens. In a July 2014 interview, Cox told Matthew Breen of *Advocate* magazine, "In black communities, all the black men are going to jail or they're gay—this is what I heard growing up." She and her brother were

A DEFINITION OF TERMS: GLAAD

GLAAD defines "transgender" as "an umbrella term for people whose gender identity and/or gender expression differs from what is typically associated with the sex they were assigned at birth." Transgender is an adjective, and it is often written with an asterisk (trans*) to demonstrate its inclusive nature.

Other terms should also be considered. Biological sex, for instance, describes an individual's anatomical features and secondary sex characteristics. It is different than

The blue, white, and pink transgender pride flag is held up by marchers during a transgender pride march in Istanbul, Turkey, on June 21, 2015.

gender identity, which is a person's inner sense of being male, female, both, neither, or gender fluid. While many people assume that we are born with our gender, it is actually something we identify with. Cisgender is a term for those people whose gender identity corresponds to the gender they were assigned at birth. Gender identity is different than sexual orientation.

Sexual orientation describes to whom a person is attracted. Transgender and cisgender people alike can identify as gay, straight, bisexual, asexual, pansexual, or any other sexual orientation.

Gender expression describes how one communicates their gender to other people. It is a combination of a person's name, the pronouns they prefer to be identified with, behavior, clothing, hair and makeup, and physical traits. Gender non-conforming describes people whose gender expression is different from traditional male and female gender expressions. Not all trans people are gender non-conforming, and not all gender non-conforming are trans.

The use of proper terminology is important, as it shows respect for and an understanding of members of the transgender community. While many cisgender people assume that being transgender is a deviation from the norm—an outlook known as a cisnormativity—everybody's gender identity and gender expression is normal and should be treated as such. In 2013, the American Psychiatric Association (APA) replaced its outdated "gender identity disorder" definition, which classified being transgender as a disorder, with "gender dysphoria." The new definition, published in the fifth edition of the *Diagnostic and Statistical Manual of Mental Disorders*, instead addresses the distress that results from "a marked difference between the individual's expressed/experienced gender and the gender others would assign him or her."

encouraged to be "new black patriarchs...shining examples of what black men should be." But Laverne didn't feel male; even as a young child, she identified with a traditionally female gender expression. Her mannerisms reflected this, and she was often bullied by her classmates.

BULLYING

Laverne was often bullied and called names because she didn't act, walk, or talk the way that other kids expected her to. Children would chase her home almost every day after school. Laverne was a fast runner, and they rarely caught up to her. However, on the days when they did, she took a beating. This was the case one particular day, an incident Laverne now recounts often on her speaking engagements as an advocate for transgender youth.

Laverne, who was a middle school student at the time, was riding the bus home. After she got off the bus, a group of children chased her down. Four or five of them caught up to her, held her down, and began hitting her with drumsticks. A parent witnessed the fight and called the school principal. Laverne was scared, not because she'd been bullied to such a violent degree, but because her mother had been called. She had kept these bullying incidents from her mother to avoid getting into trouble. Gloria Cox thought that her child should stand up for herself. She even scolded Laverne, claiming that she should have fought back against the bullies. Laverne was scared that her mother wouldn't love her because of her femininity. She didn't believe that her mother would appreciate her authentic self: a girl who thought better of herself than fighting in the schoolyard.

To make up for the bullying she experienced in middle school, Laverne worked hard to earn straight As. Yet, school was not enjoyable. She didn't have a lot of friends and filled her time with television and books. She liked entertaining shows such as the popular 1980s musical TV series *Fame* and *Solid Gold*. Both featured singing and dancing. The youngster was known for mimicking the choreography she watched on the shows. The library was Laverne's favorite hangout. She read books on a variety of subjects: self-help, sexuality, and history. She also loved biographies that detailed the lives of black artists, especially opera singer Leontyne Price and founder of the Dance Theatre of Harlem Arthur Mitchell.

POLICING GENDER

School children weren't the only ones to bully a young Laverne. Adults tried, as Cox now calls

Opera singer Leontyne Price was an inspiring figure to a young Laverne. Here, Price is photographed at Oprah Winfrey's Legends Ball on May 14, 2005, in Santa Barbara, California.

it, to "police her gender." One incident stands out in her mind. Laverne was in the third grade and had watched *Gone with the Wind*. The lead character, Scarlett O'Hara, had a handheld fan. When Cox when to Six Flags amusement park with a group of her fellow churchgoers, similar fans were sold at the gift shop. Laverne bought one and brought it to school. She fanned and fanned herself like Scarlett O'Hara. Her teacher saw the fan and called Laverne's mother, Gloria. The teacher told Cox, "Your son is going to end up in New Orleans wearing a dress if you don't get him into therapy right away."

Laverne was put into therapy. In therapy, Laverne expressed that she felt that she was a girl. Laverne did not continue with therapy for very long, especially after the therapist suggested testosterone injections to make Laverne behave in a more "masculine" way. Gloria pulled Laverne out of treatment permanently, but the child felt embarrassed. "Going to a therapist and the fear of God being placed in me about ending up in New Orleans wearing a dress, that was a profoundly shaming moment for me," Cox told Katy Steinmetz in a May 8, 2014, interview for *Time*. "I associated it with being some sort of degenerate, with not being successful." Laverne suppressed her feelings and put on a brave face. She threw herself into dance—and into the dream that, one day, she'd become famous.

While others were enjoying free play in physical education class, Laverne Cox was dancing to the music in her head. She danced in grocery stores, bringing the musicals of her imagination to life with footwork and shopping carts. At five years old, Laverne began begging her mother for dance classes. Sadly, the family didn't have enough money for such lessons. However, Laverne didn't give up. It took her three years, but she eventually got her mother's support. A young Laverne earned a scholarship to cover tuition for Culture in Black and White, a program for low-income families. Laverne took tap and jazz classes but not ballet, as her mother thought it to be "too gay." However, Laverne was content with any dance classes. When reflecting on the happiest moments of her childhood, Cox thinks of dancing and performing. In fact, she often says that dance saved her life.

REACHING PUBERTY

A sixth-grade Laverne fully expected to develop secondary sex characteristics associated with young women when she reached puberty. Such characteristics include breasts and menstruation.

SUICIDE RATES IN THE TRANSGENDER COMMUNITY

According to "Suicide Attempts Among Transgender and Gender Non-Conforming Adults: Findings of the National Transgender Discrimination Survey" (NTDS), 41 percent of transgender and gender non-conforming people reported having attempted suicide in their lifetime. This number is especially alarming when compared to the much lower statistics of 10–20 percent of cisgender gay, lesbian, and bisexual adults who reported having attempted suicide and the mere 4.6 percent of the overall US public who reported having attempted suicide.

Why is the attempted suicide rate so much higher for members of the transgender community? The NTDS attributes high suicide rates to untreated mental health issues (which may include depression) as well as discrimination, harassment, and violence.

If you or a loved one has ever considered suicide, there is help. You are not alone. Trans Lifeline is a hotline that helps transgender individuals in crisis. It is staffed "by transgender people for transgender people." Trans Lifeline offers free, knowledgeable, and confidential services to those who have questions about their gender identity, experience gender dysphoria, or may be considering suicide. Trans Lifeline can be reached in the United States at (877) 565-8860 and in Canada at (877) 330-6366.

However, to Laverne's disappointment, she developed secondary sex characteristics typically associated with young men. Around this time, Laverne also recognized her strong attraction to boys. This attraction defied the teachings that she had learned in church—that being attracted to other members of the same sex was a sin (Laverne did not yet outwardly express her gender identity as a woman) and that she'd go to hell. Laverne imagined that her grandmother—who had recently passed—was looking down from heaven with disappointment. She began to feel that everything about herself was shameful, sinful, and disgusting.

Laverne grew so distraught thinking that she wasn't who she was "supposed" to be that, at one point, she headed for the household medicine cabinet. Laverne reached for a bottle of pills and swallowed the contents in an attempt at suicide. She fell asleep, and when she finally woke up, she experienced an awful stomachache. Laverne was upset that she had survived and vowed to squelch her attraction to boys.

Laverne did not tell her family about her failed suicide attempt. Her mother had been dealing with the pressures of being a working mother, and her brother had been involved in the details of his own life. Laverne felt alone. To cope, she began overachieving. Not only did she continue to earn straight As, but she also became a member of the National Junior Honor Society, an academic organization that recognizes outstanding students in grades six through eight. She was a public speaking champion in the eighth grade. She was also elected vice president of the student council at Palmer Pillans Middle School.

CHAPTER 2

JOURNEY TO WOMANHOOD

Opportunity came knocking the day Laverne Cox learned about the Alabama School of Fine Arts (ASFA) in Birmingham, Alabama. The ASFA is a public school that offers core academics as well as six college-level specialties for students in grades seven through twelve: creative writing, dance, math and science, music, theater arts, and visual arts. In Laverne's mind, the ASFA was the real-life version of *Fame*, her favorite television show about a New York City performing arts high school.

Although admission was very competitive, Laverne knew she had to apply. The only problem she faced was that ASFA's dance program was a ballet-only program. She had only studied tap and jazz. But Laverne came up with a plan. She'd been writing and decided to apply for the creative writing program. Once accepted, she would catch up on ballet and transfer to the dance program. Her plan worked. At age fourteen, Laverne was awarded a scholarship to ASFA. Her brother, Reginald, was also accepted. ASFA was about four hours north of the twins' hometown, so they moved onto campus.

HIGH SCHOOL: AN EXPLORATION OF GENDER IDENTITY

For the first time, Laverne experienced shame regarding her race and social class at ASFA. Other students were from other races and affluent families; she and Reginald were two of only three African American students in the dorms. The twins felt discriminated against at times. In addition, Laverne first began to understand her gender identity. In a July 2014 interview, Cox told Matthew Breen of *Advocate* magazine, "I definitely did not identify as male, but I didn't identify as a woman yet either, not until later. I started wearing culottes and bell-bottoms and makeup. I was very androgynous in high school, and continued in college."

"A GIRL BRAIN, BUT A BOY BODY"

Despite being assigned male at birth in 2000, Jazz Jennings has always known that she was a girl. Her family was very supportive of her gender identity. When she started kindergarten, her family supported her decision to publicly express her gender identity as female. Unfortunately, not everyone was so supportive of Jazz. When she was eight years old, she was banned from her local girls' soccer team by league officials. After a two-and-a-half-year legal battle, the United States Soccer Federation adopted a trans-inclusive policy.

Today, Jazz is a well-known activist for trans youth. She co-authored *I Am Jazz* with Jessica Herthel. This children's picture book is loosely based on Jazz's real-life experiences and advocates for trans youth. Jazz also speaks publicly, addressing audiences at schools, conferences, conventions, universities, and medical schools nationwide. She has been featured on 20/20 by Barbara Walters, *Katie* with Katie Couric, *Dr. Drew, The Rosie Show,* and in an Oprah Winfrey Network Documentary, *I Am Jazz: A Family in Transition.*

Jazz is an honorary co-founder of the TransKids Purple Rainbow Foundation, an organization that advocates for trans youth and provides scholarships for young people to attend trans-friendly camps. In 2013, Jazz founded Purple Rainbow Tails. Through this organization, Jazz creates and sells customized,

Jazz Jennings appears at the TrevorLIVE Gala on December 6, 2015, in Los Angeles, California.

sculpted, silicone mermaid tails. She donates a portion of the proceeds to the TransKids Purple Rainbow Foundation. Jazz has also received many awards for her activism, including the Colin Higgins Youth Courage Award, and she appeared on *Time* magazine's list of the "Top 25 Most Influential Teens" in 2014. In 2015, TLC produced an eleven-part reality series on Jazz and her family's life titled *I Am Jazz*.

Along with her advocacy, Jazz does what typical teenagers do. She hangs out with friends, draws, plays sports, and binge watches her favorite films and TV shows. She loves math, science, and writing, and hopes to one day pursue these career options.

Despite being bullied for rejecting others' notions of her identity, Laverne took the initiative to define her own gender identity. She wanted to find her place in the world and make others happy so they could be proud of her. In the end, the androgyny wasn't satisfying. However, it did help her on her journey to become who she is today.

A HIGHER EDUCATION

Laverne Cox graduated seventh in her class from the ASFA and accepted a dance scholarship to Indiana University in Bloomington, Indiana. There, she studied ballet. However, this classical style had very distinct gender roles. Men danced male roles, and women danced female roles. Cox was consistently cast in male roles and no longer felt comfortable with this convention. While at Indiana University, she began to experiment with her gender expression. She wore makeup, shaved her head, and sported Mohawks.

After two years, Cox transferred to Marymount Manhattan College in New York City. It was there that Cox's love for acting blossomed. She shared in a March 2012 article for *The Huffington Post* that a "guest instructor by the name of Daniel Banks saw me walking down the hall in all my androgyny and said, 'I want you in my play.'" The play was Max Frisch's *Andorra*, a post–World War II play about anti-Semitism. Cox played the part of "Village Idiot." Cox recalls, "The idiot in this play has no lines but simply grins and nods. Everyone said I stole the play, with no lines…At least that's how I remember it." Cox changed majors from dance to theater.

It was at Marymount Manhattan College (shown here) that Laverne Cox discovered her love for acting.

During her senior year, Cox scored her first film role. She had been on the subway wearing a vintage paisley coat with a fur collar. She had box braids, and her makeup was heavy with fake eyelashes and shaved eyebrows. A woman approached Cox, believing that she'd be ideal for her movie project. Cox ended up auditioning for the role, and she got the part. While she does share the story of being cast, Cox doesn't share details about the movie or its title as the film depicts her prior to her public transition from male to female. Cox completed her studies at Marymount and earned a bachelor of fine arts in theater.

JOURNEY TO WOMANHOOD

Some transgender people can remember a distinct moment when they first articulated their gender identity. For Laverne Cox, however, her journey felt more like a gradual evolution. It began in childhood and came to fruition after she moved to New York City. The city's nightclub scene welcomed self-expression, allowing Cox to outwardly express how she felt. In what she calls her thrift shop "Salvation Armani" outfits, she would walk to the front of lines waiting to get into clubs and could enter without question. It was the first time she'd been celebrated for her gender expression. Cox felt like a celebrity.

Cox also began meeting transgender women. This was a new concept for her. She'd heard of being transgender before, but members of the transgender community had always been poorly portrayed or outright misrepresented in the media. Popular television shows such as *All in the Family* (1971–1979) and *The Jeffersons* (1975–1985) had featured trans characters in story lines, but there were no trans characters on television shown as successful, accomplished members of society. Cox had not known any transgender people personally until she met Tina Sparkles, an African American trans woman, at a nightclub. The two became friendly, and over time, Cox watched her friend transition into an elegant woman. Sparkles's success, sophistication, and elegance impressed Cox, and all of the misconceptions she had held about transgender people disappeared. She knew that if Sparkles could transition and find acceptance, so, too, could she. Cox began to express her gender as a woman at all times.

Later, Cox changed her name and began using female gender pronouns—"she," "her," and "herself." She made a doctor's appointment to

Generally recognized for its inclusion of underrepresented or controversial subject matter, *The Jeffersons* featured a character who was a trans woman in the October 1977 episode "Once a Friend."

begin hormone therapy, a medical step some transgender individuals take as part of their transition. She began to identify openly as a trans woman. It was a relief for Cox to own such an identity. In her July 2014 article for the *Advocate*, Cox said, "I feel like it was something I'd been running away from my whole life. Something I'd been fighting and trying not to be and trying to negotiate, instead of just trying to be who I am. It was just a relief." Despite her breakthrough and the more open

COMING OUT AS TRANSGENDER

If you are transgender and are considering coming out to your family and friends, congratulate yourself for taking this courageous step. Understand that you're under no obligation to tell anyone, but if you do, it is in your time and at your speed. You also do not have to tell everyone at once.

First, you may want to learn more about what it means to be transgender and to transition. You can educate yourself with online and in-print materials from trans-friendly organizations and medical centers (a list of several organizations is included at the end of this resource). Therapists and trans community support groups are valuable resources for the emotional, physical, and social aspects of coming out as trans. These organizations and resources can also educate you on the different steps trans people might consider as parts of their transition, including name changes, hormone therapy, gender affirmation surgery, and changing legal documents such as birth certificates, Social Security cards, and driver's licenses. But don't worry. Every person can transition on their own terms, taking the steps they choose when they're ready. Coming out is a journey that you, and only you, guide.

When you're ready, share your news with trusted friends and family members. Don't be surprised by the range of emotions (happiness, relief, anger, confusion, anxiety, and fear) you might receive. Give your loved ones time to process the news. Most likely it took you time to realize your gender identity, and it may take them time, too. If you're a student, consider telling faculty members whom you trust. Ask them to be a part of your support system. If you have a job, consider telling your boss. Together you can come up with a timeline for your public transition at work.

New York culture she had found, bullying was still a problem for Cox. She recalls being yelled at on the streets that she was a man. Today she realizes that such statements are an act of violence and that being trans is something to celebrate.

COMING OUT TO MOM

As Laverne Cox's evolution continued, she was soon ready to share her trans breakthrough with her mother, Gloria. It took about eight months from when Cox began medical steps of her transition from male to female for her to come out to her mother. Gloria was in denial at first, but she wanted her daughter to be in her life. Laverne gave her mother space and time to accept and feel comfortable with her daughter's transition, which she eventually did.

Gloria had some difficulty with her daughter's chosen name and preferred pronouns. The two had a number of honest conversations but approached the difficult topics with love and empathy. In addition, Gloria apologized for the bullying her daughter received as a child. She admitted to not having known what to do or how to deal with it. However, Laverne understands that her mother always loved her and that she is supportive and proud of her. Ultimately, that's all Cox wanted from her mother. Not only does Gloria Cox continue to support her daughter, but she cheers her on publicly. In fact, the elder Cox surprised her daughter by walking out on stage to celebrate her at the 25th Annual GLAAD Media Awards in April 2014.

CHAPTER 3

OWNING HER IDENTITY IN THE BIG APPLE

While pursing acting roles, Cox worked various odd jobs. She was a receptionist, served tables at a coffee shop, and cleaned the office of an acting coach in exchange for lessons. Despite a handful of small television and film roles in the early 2000s, Cox's acting career had become stale. Industry people told her that they didn't know what to do with her, despite her talent. They told her that she wouldn't find work as there were few transgender roles in major productions at that time. In fact, there were very few openly transgender actors in general, and when trans actors scored roles, they were often confined to playing transgender characters. One exception was Candis Cayne, the first openly transgender actor to

Candis Cayne appears at the Women Who GLSEN Event in Los Angeles, California, on May 1, 2011.

play a recurring role on a primetime series. She appeared in ABC's *Dirty Sexy Money* (2007).

FASHION AND HER FIRST ROLES

Laverne Cox always loved fashion. It gave her the freedom to express who she was from the inside out. While figuring out her next career move, she decided to become a designer. Cox enrolled in the prestigious Fashion Institute of Technology (FIT) in New York City. She attended for a few semesters but dropped out when she was cast as a Moroccan stripper and prostitute in the independent film *Daughter of Arabia* (2003). In the film, Cox filmed her first nude scene, a move considered by many to be very brave for somebody relatively early in her transition process. But Cox didn't mind. She was living her acting dream.

Despite leaving FIT, fashion continued to be an important part of Cox's life. She moved beyond the culottes and bell-bottoms, and began wearing body-flattering gowns and mini-dresses in bold colors, sequins, velvet, chiffon, shimmery fabrics, and exotic prints. Cox also stayed active in the fashion scene. In years since, she has attended New York City fashion shows and even later appeared as a guest judge on season four of *Project Runway: All Stars* (2014–15).

Cox sits front row at The Blonds Fashion Show in New York on September 10, 2008. Despite leaving her design studies at FIT, Cox has always maintained an interest in fashion.

While fashion had briefly called Cox away from the stage, she has always maintained that she is the happiest when she's acting. It sustains her. In a March 2012 article for *The Huffington Post*, Cox stated:

> *My entire life I have been trying to find ways to get up in front of people and perform. I have thought of giving up so many times. Having a career as an actor has often seemed impossible, silly, and misguided, particularly for my "type" [a trans woman]. In the acting business, until you're a star, you're a type. In true actor fashion, I currently don't know where my next acting job is coming from, but that's the name of the game.*

Over the years, Cox performed in student films, off-off-Broadway theater productions, and independent films. Her early television work included brief roles on *Law & Order*, *Bored to Death*, and *Law and Order: Special Victims Unit*. However, each of these roles was that of a sex worker—trans actors are often typecast for these parts. By the time Cox landed her breakout role on *Orange Is the New Black*, she had played a

HISTORY OF THE TRANSGENDER MOVEMENT

Sometimes, it seems like the fight for transgender rights is a relatively recent movement because of the spike in media coverage of transgender figures in the past several years. However, the transgender community's fight to achieve dignity, respect, and equal rights had its first milestones starting about a century ago. In 1917, Alan L. Hart, an American physician, was one of the first transgender people in the United States to undergo gender affirmation surgery. Another early trans pioneer was Christine Jorgensen, a former private in the U.S. Army who traveled to Denmark for gender affirmation surgery and hormone treatments in 1951–52. When she returned to the United States, Jorgensen became a celebrity and advocate.

In May 1959, a riot broke out when Los Angeles police attempted to arrest gay and transgender patrons for hanging out at the popular donut shop Cooper's Donuts. This uprising is considered the first LGBTQ+ uprising. In August 1966, riots erupted when police officers attempted to kick a transgender woman out of the trans-friendly Compton's Cafeteria in San Francisco. The biggest riot happened at the Stonewall Inn in New York's Greenwich Village in June 1969. New York City police raided the gay club. In response, the crowd rioted, and demonstrations lasted for days. These protests are seen as the start of LGBTQ+ movement in the United States.

Actor Otoja Abit depicts Marsha P. Johnson in the film *Stonewall* (2015).

The 1970s saw several milestones for the movement. In 1970, Stone Wall rioters and LGBTQ+ activists Sylvia Rivera and Marsha P. Johnson founded the advocacy group and shelter Street Transvestite Action Revolutionaries. In 1975, Minneapolis, Minnesota, became the first US city to prohibit transphobic discrimination. In 1977, Renée Richards, a trans woman, won a legal battle allowing her to compete at the US Open as a woman.

In 1992, the International Conference on Transgender Law and Employment Policy focused on legal issues related to employment, health care, and military service. Transgender Day of Remembrance (TDOR) was established in 1999. In 2014, Medicare lifted a long-standing ban on preventive care and medically necessary hormone therapy and gender affirmation surgery for transgender patients. In December 2014, the Equal Employment Opportunity Commission ruled that Title VII of the 1964 Civil Rights Act made it illegal to discriminate based on sex, thus protecting transgender employees. Today, the fight for equal protection continues as state legislatures debate over controversial "bathroom bills," which deny trans students access to the bathrooms corresponding to their gender identity.

sex worker seven times in various student films and television series. Each time, though, she tried to bring something new to the role.

Cox did get to move beyond sex worker roles. For example, in 2012 she landed the role of Chantelle, a disabled African American transgender woman, in the film *Musical Chairs.* It was a love story that took place in the world of wheelchair ballroom dancing. *Musical Chairs* was Cox's first film to be distributed and shown in theaters. In 2013, she won Best Supporting Actress at the Massachusetts Independent Film Festival for her role.

A DOSE OF REALITY

In 2008, VH1's reality show *I Want to Work for Diddy* offered contestants the opportunity to land a job working with rap mogul, entrepreneur, and actor Sean Combs (known variously as Diddy, P. Diddy, Puff Daddy, and Puffy). VH1.com describes the show's premise: "After an exhaustive nationwide search, VH1 found determined young men and women with the raw potential to assist and exist with one of the world's most demanding CEOs." Participants on the show's two-season run competed in challenges based on real experiences of Combs's former assistants.

Laverne Cox saw an opportunity and auditioned to be a contestant. Those closest to her thought she shouldn't do the show. They thought she would not have editorial control over her story and the way it was told on television. Like most reality shows, Combs and the production team would decide how to present Cox—possibly in a negative or mocking light.

Cox, however, was determined to do the show. She had two reasons: the first, to advance her career, and the second, because she thought it would be powerful for the trans community for a big-name rapper and businessperson to embrace a transgender woman on television. During the audition process, Cox made it clear that if she participated, the show's producers should not exploit her gender identity for ratings. She was assured that this wouldn't happen, and that Combs wanted her for her merits. He knew they could make history together, as she would be the first African American trans woman to participate on a reality competition show.

In the production phase of the show, Combs sought the advice of the president of GLAAD (formerly the Gay & Lesbian Alliance Against Defamation) on how the show should address Cox's gender identity on the show. He was advised to let Cox take the lead in telling

Sean "Diddy" Combs appears at a film premiere in New York City on December 1, 2008.

her own story. Many trans men and women contacted Cox online, inspired by this new portrayal of a trans woman of color. Cox left the show in its sixth week and did not end up working for Combs. Regardless, her participation was

HOW TO BE AN ALLY

Being an ally to the transgender community not only helps transgender and gender non-conforming individuals feel comfortable and accepted, but it also enables you to educate other cisgender friends and family on how to respect the transgender community and understand what it means to be transgender. First, approach transgender individuals with an open heart and listening ears. Acknowledge their many identities: siblings, friends, neighbors, and coworkers. Members of the transgender community vary in age, and they come from different races, socioeconomic backgrounds, and levels of education. It is best not to assume a person's gender identity or preferred gender pronouns; some gender non-conforming people consider themselves to be both male and female, neither, or fluid. When possible, always respectfully ask how somebody wishes to be addressed.

Next, consider the importance of privacy when discussing the fact that somebody is transgender. Unless it is relevant to the conversation at hand, there's little reason to identify somebody as transgender, just as you wouldn't necessarily identify other friends based on their religion, race, or sexual orientation. Also, understand that a trans person is the best expert on their own life and experiences. Let them take the lead in coming out and telling their stories to others. Be sensitive with names and other terms. For instance, if you know a trans person's birth name, do not share it. Opt to say "assigned male at birth" or "assigned female at birth," as opposed to "born a boy" or "born a girl."

Avoid asking questions about anatomy, hormone therapy, gender affirmation surgery, and sexual practices. These are extremely private matters—for both trans and cisgender people. Also, not all transgender people can or want to pursue hormone therapy or surgery. Some are happy with a social transition alone. Each person's transition is their own. Be aware that some trans friends may not feel safe in certain public settings, particularly in restrooms or locker rooms. Have your friend's back, and be willing to do what you can to accommodate their privacy and safety.

If you have questions, educate yourself. Confront transphobic rhetoric when you hear it—as long as you're safe—as it can be oppressive and often linked to racism, sexism, and homophobia.

Cox appears with E! news editor Marc Malkin at the Homos Away from Home Party on January 24, 2011, in Park City, Utah.

a positive experience, as she became the first trans woman of color to appear on an American reality television series. Cox was awarded the GLAAD Media Award for Outstanding Reality Program. Her participation also later led to a new gig: producing and starring in another VH1 project, *TRANS-form Me*.

TRANSForm Me made Laverne Cox the first African American transgender woman to produce and star in her own television show. *TRANSForm Me* was a makeover show. Cox and costars Jamie Clayton and Nina Poon traveled across the United States in search of people in need of makeovers from the inside out. The first episode aired on March 15, 2010. Cox thought it would be her breakout role, but that wasn't the case. The final episode aired on May 3, 2010.

Cox was left wondering what her next step would be. "So I had to have a 'come to Jesus' moment and I reevaluated a lot of things in my life," Cox told Michelangelo Signorile in a June 2014 SiriusXM Progress interview. "I remember saying to my agent, 'I want to act. No more reality. I don't want to be a celebrity. I just want to act.'" Cox found a new acting coach. "I recommitted to that process and it really just became about the work. So I was hoping I would just work. I've dreamed about being on the cover of magazines, but my goal was to be a working actor."

CHAPTER 4

A ROLE OF A LIFETIME

In late 2012, Laverne Cox landed the role of her career when she was cast as Sophia Burset on Netflix's original series *Orange Is the New Black*. First aired in 2013, this prison drama was loosely based on the memoir *Orange Is the New Black: My Year in a Women's Prison* written by Piper Kerman. Kerman grew up in a middle-class family in Boston, Massachusetts. She graduated in 1992 from Smith College, a prestigious all-women's college in Northampton, Massachusetts. While waiting tables in her college town, she became romantically involved with a woman who, on their first date, shared that she was involved in an international drug trafficking ring. Kerman found this to be exciting. She and her girlfriend spent the next four months traveling the world as they worked for the trafficking ring.

In 1993, the twenty-four-year-old Kerman traveled from Chicago, Illinois, to Brussels, Belgium, carrying a suitcase of money destined for an international drug lord. She wasn't caught, but she realized that the lifestyle was far too dangerous. Kerman created a new life for herself, becoming a freelance producer in New York City and dating a new boyfriend whom she would eventually marry. However, in 1998, federal officers arrested Kerman on conspiracy drug charges related to her drug trafficking activities. She pled guilty. In 2004, Kerman surrendered

Piper Kerman (left) appears alongside actor Taylor Schilling (right), who portrays Kerman on the television adaptation of *Orange Is the New Black*, at the 2013 PaleyFest in New York City on October 2, 2013.

all of her possessions and reported to the Federal Correctional Institution, a minimum-security women's correctional facility prison in Danbury, Connecticut. While incarcerated for a year, she met an extremely diverse community of female prisoners. *Orange Is the New Black* shared her experiences.

A MOSAIC OF CHARACTERS

Television writer and producer Jenji Kohan was inspired by Piper Kerman's book. She borrowed the basic story line and fictionalized other elements to create a more diverse cast of characters. Kohan honored the community of incarcerated women by building highly dimensional characters. In an August 2013 interview with NPR, Kohan explained her approach to writing the show's characters:

> *I'm always looking for those places where you can slam really disparate people up against one another, and they have to deal with each other. There are very few crossroads anymore. We talk about this country as this big melting pot, but it's a mosaic. There's [sic] all these pieces. They're next to each other; they're not necessarily mixing. And I'm looking for*

those spaces where people actually do mix—and prison just happens to be a terrific one.

Kohan put together a very diverse cast of talented—and not necessarily well-known—actors. She presented her project to various television networks, and Netflix jumped at the opportunity to feature the show. The Internet television network beat other networks to the punch and ordered thirteen episodes.

A major part of *Orange Is the New Black*'s appeal is its diverse cast of characters played by a mix of newer and more established actors. Laverne Cox (third from left) appears here with several of her costars and the show's casting director at a screening of the show in August 2015.

One character in the show's story line was Sophia Burset, a smart and quick-witted African American transgender woman imprisoned for fraud. She works as a hairdresser in the prison beauty parlor. As the show develops, viewers learn that Sophia has a wife outside prison named Crystal. Together, the couple has a son, Michael, who has difficulty accepting that his father has come out as a transgender woman. Flashback scenes show the strained relationship between Sophia and her family as they adapt to her transition from male to female.

In one flashback, Sophia and her son, Michael, go shoe shopping. When considering the purchase of an expensive pair of sneakers, Michael spots Sophia's wallet, full of stolen credit cards that had been used to pay for expensive gender affirmation surgery. It is later revealed that Michael was the one who informed the police, leading to Sophia's arrest and incarceration.

The role of Sophia Burset proved to be a bit of a challenge for Kohan and the show's casting director, Jennifer Euston. They wanted a transgender actor who could accurately depict Sophia's in-depth relationship challenges with family and fellow inmates. Kohan wanted someone who could do the character justice and knew firsthand the challenges of transitioning and maintaining a close relationship with their family. Euston had previously auditioned Cox for another project, but the actor did not get the role. She did, however, nail the audition for *Orange Is the New Black*. Cox had no idea that Sophia Burset would be her breakout role. In fact, no one expected that the show and its characters would become such a massive hit.

Right before signing on with Netflix's *Orange*, Cox had gone eight months without an acting job. She was on a payment plan to pay rent for her New York City apartment. Even with her new contract she wasn't

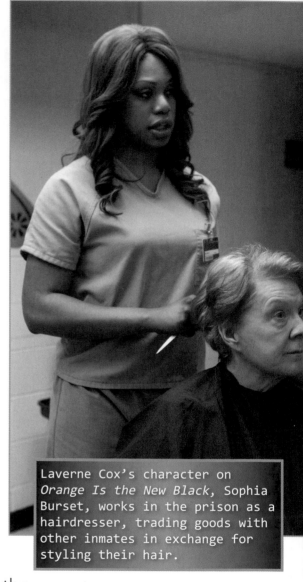

Laverne Cox's character on *Orange Is the New Black*, Sophia Burset, works in the prison as a hairdresser, trading goods with other inmates in exchange for styling their hair.

taking any chances. Cox kept her day job at Lucky Cheng's, a restaurant in New York's Lower East Side neighborhood. Lucky Cheng's was known for its drag-queen servers and entertainers. Cox had initially applied to serve tables but soon after began entertaining patrons as a drag queen. Cox never truly was a drag queen—which is generally a cisgender man who dresses as a woman for a performance—but chose to play the role for the sake of employment (as some transgender women do). While she was thankful to have the job, Cox found playing a drag queen to be degrading. Nevertheless, the people she worked with were like a family to her, and she continued to work at Lucky Cheng's until July 2013—when *Orange Is the New Black* premiered.

TELLING POWERFUL STORIES

Laverne Cox considers the role of Sophia Burset to be a gift. In interviews, she has explained how she relates to many of the challenges Sophia faces. "I think a lot of us have been in relationships where being authentically true to ourselves might be in conflict with being in that relationship," Cox told *The Telegraph* in June 2015. Although Cox's life isn't the same as Sophia's, the actor works to honor the stages of Sophia's transition with each powerful episode.

In season one, episode three, "Lesbian Request Denied," we get a look into Sophia's past. Before transitioning, Sophia was a firefighter who stole personal information to commit credit card fraud. We see her life at that time, where she lives publicly as a firefighter and husband, but at home tries on lacey bras and women's underwear. It's an early look into the buildup before the character came out to her family as a trans woman.

In other scenes, we see Sophia explaining prison bathroom use and other quirks of life in prison to the show's lead character, Piper. She offers advice, including accessorizing with limited resources. The prison commissary doesn't stock size thirteen shower slippers, so Sophia fashions her own out of silver duct tape. While modeling them for Piper, Sophia proudly claims that they're couture, noting, "Metallics are very in this season."

Not all of Sophia's scenes are so light-hearted. In other scenes, Cox's character goes to collect her hormone pills in order to maintain her hormone therapy, only to learn that the prison is no longer able to provide brand-name—and therefore, more expensive and better quality—hormones. She's given a generic

Certain episodes of *Orange Is the New Black* have highlighted the discrimination that trans prisoners face. In the season three episode "Don't Make Me Come Back There," Sophia is attacked by a fellow inmate and the guards do not have the proper training to adequately protect her.

alternative. Sophia meets with a prison official, pleading to get back on her prescribed hormone medications in order to avoid hot flashes, night sweats, and the regrowth of body hair. She asks to see the prison doctor, but she is told her situation isn't an emergency. Cox then takes a bobble-head toy off of the official's desk, pops off the head, and swallows it. After choking it down, she says she needs to report an emergency. Sophia is then put on suicide watch by the doctor. Surprised, Sophia sets the record straight that she didn't really want to kill herself. "I've given five years, $80,000, and my freedom for this. I'm finally who I'm supposed to be. Do you understand? I can't go back," she tells the clinic doctor. The encounter highlights the ways in which medical care and government organizations don't always adequately address the medical needs of members of the transgender community.

Another flashback shows the vulnerability Sophia feels early in her transition and the relationship she has with her wife, Crystal. Cox points to it as her favorite scene—both in the show and of her acting career at large. It is what she commonly refers to as the "dressing scene." Sophia is standing in the couple's bedroom, showing her attempt to put together a stylish outfit with women's clothing. Crystal doesn't like the pieced-together look and goes to the closet to retrieve a more sophisticated dress. She helps Sophia change her clothes, and viewers can sense the deep love that still exists between the two. Sophia gives Crystal permission to leave her, but she wants to stay together. This was her family.

In an on-set interview for season two of the show, Cox shared the following about the so-called dressing scene:

> *It's just really what you dream about [as an actor] to just be able to be in a moment of sheer vulnerability and exposure with another actor. It's a moment that I think we really understand that these people deeply love each other, but she cannot lie anymore about who she is. I think whether you're transgender or not, most of us get to a point in our lives when we can no longer lie to ourselves.*

Cox wanted to play the pre-transition version of her character, and the crew spent eight hours transforming her into a man using facial hair, a do-rag, and makeup. But the episode director felt that Cox couldn't pull off the look convincingly. She took one look at Cox and decided that they'd better hire someone who

THE MEDIA'S FOCUS ON SURGERY

Transitioning from one gender to another is a process that entails several kinds of changes. It may involve social changes such as coming out as trans to loved ones, changing one's name, using specific gender pronouns, and dressing differently or taking other steps to alter gender expression; medical changes such as beginning hormone therapy or undergoing a gender affirmation surgery; or legal changes such as obtaining a new driver's license, passport, or Social Security card. Which steps a person chooses to take as part of their transition depends on the person. Some trans people may not want to or feel the need to go through every aforementioned step. Some also cannot take certain steps—particularly the medical and legal ones—for financial reasons. Regardless, a person's gender identity is in no way dependent upon any such steps.

With this being said, many cisgender people wonder about the medical steps of transitioning, and the media often focuses on this curiosity. Media sources highlight gender affirmation surgery in its stories and interviews. However, this tendency often overemphasizes the procedure and objectifies the transgender community. Medical procedures are private matters between a patient and a doctor. Unless a transgender celebrity chooses to publicly address their transition and any surgeries they've undergone as part of it, focus on the topic is rude and harmful. Furthermore, an undue spotlight on anatomy can undermine the validity of a person's transgender identity.

Cox chooses not to talk about surgery, anatomy, or her own transition in public. She prefers to focus on the lack of press coverage on major issues that affect the transgender community, such as the staggering rates of suicide among trans youth and discrimination and violence against the trans.

looked more masculine. Cox then contacted her twin brother, Reginald (who had also harnessed his artistic talent as a musician, performing under the stage name M. Lamar). He auditioned for and scored the role.

AND THE AWARD GOES TO...

Orange Is the New Black has received numerous awards, including TV Program of the Year at the American Film Institute (AFI) Awards (2014), Best Comedy Series at the Critics' Choice Television Awards (2014), Outstanding Performance by an Ensemble in a Comedy Series at the Screen

Actors Guild (SAG) Awards (2015 and 2016), Outstanding Comedy Series at the GLAAD Media Awards (2014), a Peabody Award (2014), and Favorite Streaming Series and Favorite Dramedy at the People's Choice Awards (2014 and 2015, respectively). Specific cast members have also been nominated for and won numerous awards.

Cox, too, has been honored for her role on the show. She received a Critic's Choice TV Award nomination for Best Supporting Actress

Laverne Cox and several of her costars hold their awards for Outstanding Performance by an Ensemble in a Comedy Series at the 21st Annual Screen Actors Guild Awards in Los Angeles, California, on January 25, 2015.

(2014), a Dorian Rising Star Award (2013–2014), and a 2014 Primetime Emmy Award nomination for Outstanding Guest Actor in a Comedy Series. The last nomination made her the first openly trans person to be nominated for an acting award in the Emmy's history. Cox was also nominated for a 2015 NAACP Image Award for Outstanding Supporting Actor in a Comedy Series.

CHAPTER 5

"JUSTICE IS WHAT LOVE LOOKS LIKE IN PUBLIC"

Today, the media and society at large have been embracing the transgender community and shining a spotlight on transgender rights like never before. "But in terms of the day-to-day lives of trans people," says Laverne Cox in a June 2015 interview with the *Telegraph*, "we still experience violence at a disproportionate rate, as well as homelessness, unemployment, the denial of health care, and being criminalized and incarcerated." With the platform provided by her celebrity, Cox has felt compelled to advocate for all members of the trans community.

"AIN'T I A WOMAN?"

Even with her own level of achievement, Laverne Cox still faces discrimination. She has felt unsafe in

DISCRIMINATION AGAINST THE TRANS COMMUNITY

In 2011, the National Center for Transgender Equality and the National Gay and Lesbian Task Force published "Injustice at Every Turn: A Report of the National Transgender Discrimination Survey." The report summarized the experiences of 6,450 transgender and gender non-conforming participants, ages eighteen to eighty-nine, from throughout the United States. Following are some of the report's findings:

• Of participants who were students in grades K–12, 78 percent reported in-school harassment, 35 percent reported physical assault, and 12 percent reported sexual violence. Fifteen percent reported having dropped out as a result of harassment.

• Ninety percent of participants all ages reported on-the-job harassment, mistreatment, or discrimination, or having taken actions to hide who they were so to avoid such treatment. Forty-seven percent reported having been fired, not hired, or denied a promotion because of their gender identity. Sixteen percent reported engaging in sex work or drug dealing in order to survive.

• Nineteen percent of participants had been refused housing and 11 percent had been evicted because of their gender identity.

• Nineteen percent were refused medical attention. (This rate was even higher among racial minorities.)

Half had to educate medical professionals about transgender care.

- Twenty-nine percent of participants reported having been harassed and/or disrespected by law enforcement, while 12 percent were either harassed by or denied equal treatment from judges or court officials.
- Fifty-seven percent of those surveyed reported having been rejected when they came out as transgender to their family.

Despite the mistreatment, participants showed great perseverance in the face of harassment and discrimination. Seventy-six percent overcame obstacles to obtaining health care in order to get hormone therapy, and 22 percent of those between ages twenty-five and forty-four who had not finished school returned to school at later ages. After transitioning, 78 percent of trans participants felt safer at work and more effective at their jobs.

public places. Cox often shares a story of heading out to buy a scarf for her final interview for *I Want to Work for Diddy* when a group of men passed her by, throwing out transphobic slurs. One man even kicked her. Scared, Cox ducked into a store. The police were called, but by the time they arrived, the men had disappeared. Cox felt empowered by calling the police, and she is thankful that this is the worst harassment she's experienced. Other members of the transgender community have faced far worse violence. Cox shares her story to educate others. She is always quick to note that her voice isn't the only voice, but she believes that hers can make a difference. Then, and only then, does her fame mean something.

One of the best ways to affect long-term change is to educate others, especially young people. Laverne Cox accomplishes this by going on speaking tours of universities across the United States and Canada. She draws attention to important issues affecting the transgender community with her speech "Ain't I a Woman? My Journey to Womanhood." It echoes those famous words spoken by Sojourner Truth, a former slave and activist for women's rights. Truth issued the question, "Ain't I a woman?" while addressing a crowd at the Women's Convention in Akron, Ohio, on May 29, 1851. (The same month and date as Cox's birthday.) Truth called for men to treat all women with respect, regardless of their skin color.

In Cox's speech, she opens, "I stand before you this evening a proud African American transgender woman." She explains that

The title of Cox's speech "Ain't I a Woman? My Journey to Womanhood" references a famous speech made by another Black pioneer for women's rights, Sojourner Truth.

she has multiple identities: that of an actor, a sister, and a daughter. She points out that she isn't one thing alone, and neither are members of her audience. Cox publicly claims her multiples identities with pride, something that she wasn't always able to do. She goes on to detail the shame she'd felt over some of her identities, namely being black, having grown up working-class, and being transgender.

Cox's speech seamlessly ties her personal experiences with the discrimination that the trans community at large faces. Cox calls for justice, repeating political activist Cornel West's quote: "Never forget that justice is what love looks like in public." She expresses concern that the biggest obstacle most trans people face is simply to being seen and accepted as the gender with which they identify. Using her hands to outline her figure, she asks crowds, "But ain't I a woman?" Interestingly enough, Cox was named Woman of the Year by *Glamour* magazine in 2014.

While on tour, Cox fulfilled the prophecy of her third-grade teacher, Ms. Ridgeway. She ended up in New Orleans wearing a dress—a green and black one—to share her lecture with students, staff, and faculty at Tulane University on February 17, 2014.

Laverne Cox speaks at The University of Connecticut's Jorgensen Center for the Performing Arts on April 22, 2015.

THE GLOBAL TRANS COMMUNITY

Before the Internet, members of the trans community were often restricted to socializing in the few locations that accepted transgender patrons. Accurate information and resources were limited. Today, acceptance is more widespread. The Internet makes it possible for trans people to network more easily and discover resources and referrals for health and wellness services. They can also find inspiration from pioneers who have been outspoken advocates for the transgender community. Perhaps the most famous transgender celebrity in recent years has been Caitlyn Jenner.

Jenner was well known as an Olympic gold medalist and reality television star prior to publicly transitioning from male to female. In 2015, Jenner came out as transgender and made waves in the media. That July, she was honored with the Arthur Ashe Courage Award at the ESPY Awards in Los Angeles, California. Later that year *Glamour* magazine named her a Woman of the Year.

"I am so moved by all the love and support Caitlyn is receiving," Cox wrote regarding Jenner's coming out and the positive reaction in a June 2015 post on her Tumblr. "It feels like a new day, indeed, when a trans person can present her authentic self to the world for the first time and be celebrated for it so universally." Cox also began using the hashtag #TransIsBeautiful. It welcomed stories from within and in support of the trans community. The hashtag also creates a space in social media for conversation, similar to the safe space Cox previously found

Television star and transgender activist Caitlyn Jenner speaks on stage at the Point Foundation's Annual Voices On Point Gala in Los Angeles, California, on October 3, 2015.

in New York City's nightlife. It was in that space that Cox had met other trans women and where her misconceptions about being transgender slipped away.

Cox continues to express concern about the privilege that she and others trans celebrities have. Others members of the trans community don't always have the wealth, fame, or resources to achieve the acceptance people such as Jenner and herself have achieved. With #TransIsBeautiful, Cox hopes to promote inner and outer beauty and, more important, acceptance for all members of her community.

BRINGING THE DISCUSSION TO MAINSTREAM MEDIA

After the success of *Orange Is the New Black*, Laverne Cox became an in-demand guest on mainstream television shows including *Good Morning America*, *The View*, *Inside Edition*, and *Conan*. She often discusses current and future projects, as well as advocacy for the trans community. When necessary, Cox boldly, and yet kindly, corrects her esteemed hosts when they innocently or unknowingly use incorrect or offensive language. For example, Cox corrected host Gayle King's wording when the latter said, "So, you were born a boy..." on *CBS This Morning* on July 29, 2014. Cox kindly explained, "Well, I was assigned male at birth…The gender thing is something that someone imposes on you. So I was assigned male at birth, but I always felt like a girl."

While appearing on *Katie* on January 6, 2014, Cox politely declined answering a genitalia-related question from host Katie Couric. Cox thought the preoccupation with transitioning does two things: first, it objectifies trans women, and second, it distracts others from addressing more important issues such as the disproportionate amount of violence faced by the trans community.

In May of that year, Cox shared her thoughts on the on-show confrontation in an interview with *Time* magazine:

> *As many people who have been on daytime TV, I've never heard someone push back and really talk about the homicide rate in the trans community and talk about the disproportionate discrimination and talk about someone like Islan Nettles, who lost her life just because she was walking down the street while trans. And to shift the narrative away from transition and surgery. I've never seen someone*

Katie Couric appears during Mercedes-Benz Fashion Week in New York City on February 7, 2014. That year, Couric had Cox as a guest on her show twice to bring awareness to trans subjects.

challenge that narrative on television before. But in the community, we've been talking about this and frustrated for years.

In June, Katie Couric invited Cox to return as a guest on the show. Cox praised Couric on her willingness to learn the appropriate dialogue when discussing trans issues. Cox also took the opportunity to explain that there is not one universal trans experience. Each trans individual experiences their gender in a unique way, and they should always take the lead in sharing their own story.

CHAPTER 6

THE BEST IS YET TO COME

Laverne Cox admits to being a work in progress. She's picked herself apart her entire life, which is difficult to imagine as she exudes confidence in her performances, guest appearances, and speaking tours. In the June/July 2015 feature in *Bust* magazine, Cox said:

> *It's a lot of spiritual work for me as I deal with and figure out how to be a famous person who's recognized. A lot of my work is to stay grounded, is to stay spiritual. It is to disconnect from what other people say about me, but also to try and be connected to the joy and the love. I think this is where I'm struggling now.*

Cox's internal work involves the shame she began to feel as a child. It's an everyday practice for her to stay in the moment and not revert back to being a bullied eight-year-old. Cox counts herself fortunate to have a skill set to deal with insecurities when they pop up. She also feels blessed to have the love, support, and validation of loved ones, whom Cox is quick to acknowledge for having helped her get to where she is today.

Susan Batson, her acting coach of five years, changed her life. Batson believed in Cox and challenged her to do the work of being an actor. Batson was also the one who told Cox that acting could change the perceptions of others. Cox carried this lesson with her as she advocated for the trans community. Brad Calcaterra, the acting coach Cox began working with in 2010, got the actor to do the deep emotional work needed to continue developing her talent.

When speaking of her agent, Paul Hilepo, Cox gets emotional. After Candis Cayne had her breakthrough role on primetime television, Cox mailed five hundred postcards to talent reps. She got four appointments from her efforts, one of which was with Paul Hilepo. Even though the meeting was not a smashing success, Hilepo saw something in Cox. He signed her and continues to represent the actor today. With the support of these important people, Cox has become who she is and uses her platform to speak for others.

FREE CECE

Cox has long been passionate about bringing awareness to violence against the trans community and the mass incarceration of trans women. This was true even before her role as Sophia Burset on *Orange Is the New Black*. The case of CeCe McDonald is one that particularly caught her attention and interest. McDonald is an African American trans woman who spent nineteen months of a forty-one-month sentence in a men's prison in St. Cloud, Minnesota.

McDonald's story began one June night in 2011. She was walking to a grocery store with four friends when a group at a dive bar began yelling discriminatory slurs at her. A physical altercation broke out, and in an effort to defend herself, McDonald stabbed an assailant who was attacking her. McDonald was injured, and the man died. In 2012, McDonald was convicted of second-degree manslaughter. Controversially, McDonald was assigned to serve her sentence not in a women's prison but in a men's prison.

Supporters of CeCe McDonald gather in downtown Minneapolis, Minnesota, on June 4, 2012, to show support for McDonald.

Cox heard about McDonald's case in a news report. She related to it personally, thinking that she easily could have been CeCe, incarcerated for defending herself against a transphobic attacker. In December 2013, Cox began production of a documentary titled *FREE CeCe*. The film brings greater awareness to McDonald's case and the ways in which trans women of color face higher incarceration rates and greater societal discrimination than other

TRANSGENDER DAY OF REMEMBRANCE

"Every two weeks, on average, someone is murdered in the United States in an act of anti-transgender violence," writes Gwendolyn Ann Smith in a November 2013 Gay Voices article for *The Huffington Post*. Smith is a transgender advocate, columnist, managing editor for the website Genderfork, and founder of the Transgender Day of Remembrance (TDOR). Smith continues, "Internationally, you see these murders happening as a near-daily occurrence."

The inspiration for TDOR was Rita Hester, a trans woman of color from Boston, Massachusetts. Hester was stabbed multiple times in her apartment on November 28, 1998. Upon arrival at the hospital, Hester was declared dead. Her murderer was never found, and to date, the case remains unsolved. Hester's story caught the attention of Smith, who had been active on America Online's transgender community forum. Also on the forum were people from Boston, Massachusetts. They recalled a similarity between Hester's story and that of Chanelle Pickett, another trans woman who had been murdered three years earlier. Sadly, though, many had forgotten Pickett's death. To remember victims of anti-trans violence, Smith started "Remembering Our Dead" in 1998. It was an online chronicle of cases of violence against members of the transgender community dating back to the 1970s that had been either ignored or misrepresented by the media.

In 1999, Smith organized the first TDOR event in San Francisco, while a second event was coordinated on the same night in Boston. Word spread online, and further TDOR events were held in other parts of the country in the years to follow. International activists and allies began hosting TDOR events in their hometowns. Today, TDOR continues to honor Hester as well as all others who have lost their lives to anti-transgender violence. It is celebrated annually on November 20 with memorials and candlelight vigils around the world.

minority groups. Cox also discusses McDonald's story in interviews and at her speaking engagements.

MOVING BEYOND SEX WORKERS: NEW ROLES

Cox has moved beyond playing the roles of sex workers. She has taken on new projects, playing the aspiring personal stylist Sheena on Fox's *The Mindy Project*, the Pulitzer Prize–winning war journalist Adele Northrop on Bravo's *Girlfriend's Guide to Divorce*, and the school drama department director Margot on MTV's *Faking It*. Cox

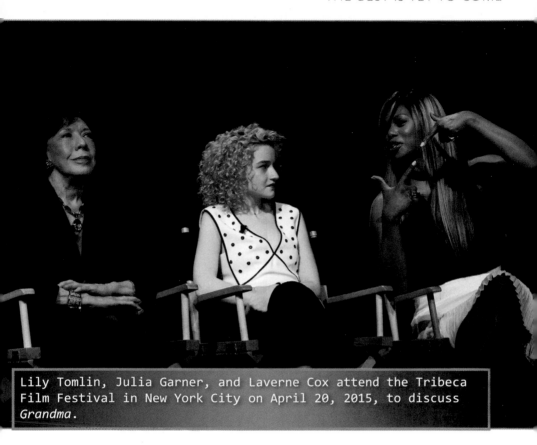

Lily Tomlin, Julia Garner, and Laverne Cox attend the Tribeca Film Festival in New York City on April 20, 2015, to discuss *Grandma*.

also played the trans Ivy League–educated lawyer Cameron Wirth on CBS's legal drama *Doubt*.

In addition to new acting roles, Cox produced and hosted a joint effort by Logo and MTV, *Laverne Cox Presents: The T Word*. The documentary, which first aired in October 2014, showed the lives of four American trans teenagers. Each of the documentary's subjects told their story about coming out and living as trans. On April 24, 2015, the documentary won Outstanding Special Class

TRUE ACTIVISM

"True activism is getting up in the morning, knowing you're living your authentic self," says Gina Bigham, program coordinator for the cultural arts and education at the Los Angeles LGBT Center. "That authenticity has the power to propel one to heights of confidence and empowerment that many in our society will never achieve. It's this power that changes the perceptions of those outside of the trans community."

Bigham, herself, is a transgender woman and an advocate in her local community. She explains:

Going through transition is not easy. In fact, it's probably the hardest thing you'll ever do. This is where you'll encounter the good, the bad, and the ugly. But with patience and perseverance, you'll crawl through your river of filth, and come out clean on the other side. Once you get to that other side, you'll find a confidence and empowerment that will take you anywhere you want to go in this life.

In her capacity as program coordinator at the LGBT Center, Bigham is the lead organizer for Trans Pride LA, and she's organized speaking events with transgender public figures—including Laverne Cox.

"You don't have to be a rattler to be an activist," says Bigham. "Just stay true to you. Being transgender is like being left-handed. It's not abnormal; it's just different. If we can share this with others, and own who we are, then we change minds, one person at a time."

Special at the 42nd Annual Daytime Creative Arts Emmy Awards.

In 2015, Cox made her way onto the silver screen as the tattoo artist Deathy in the major motion picture *Grandma*, starring Lily Tomlin. In 2016, Cox scored the role of Dr. Frank-N-Furter, the transvestite alien character originally played by Tim Curry in *The Rocky Horror Picture Show* (1975), for a Fox television remake of the cult classic.

A TRUE ADVOCATE AND PIONEER

On April 12, 2014, Laverne Cox was presented with the Stephen F. Kolzak Award at the 25th Annual GLAAD Media Awards in Los Angeles. The award honors a media professional who has furthered equality for the LGBTQ community. Past recipients include other LGBTQ activists such as Chaz Bono and Ellen DeGeneres.

Laverne Cox speaks at the 26th Annual GLAAD Media Awards in New York City on May 9, 2015.

While accepting the award, Cox said, "I'm still not used to getting awards. I'm an African American, transgender woman from a working-class background raised by a single mother. We are not programmed to think we should receive these kinds of awards—but I like to think that things are changing." Cox has publicly acknowledged that winning these awards isn't about her; she believes it's about the trans community at large. It gives a voice to other transgender people.

Cox's other awards for her activism include a Courage Award from the Anti-Violence Project in 2013 and New York City's LGBT Community Center's Community Leader Award (an honor that subsequently led to Cox being the 2014 Grand Marshal for NYC Pride).

In addition to awards, Cox has been recognized for her activism and influence in magazines. In June 2014, she graced the cover of *Time*. The shot made her the first openly transgender person to be featured on the magazine's cover in the magazine's history. Later, in 2015, Cox made *Time*'s list of the "100 Most Influential People." Cox's advocacy earned her other highly coveted magazine covers, including the May 2015 issue of *Variety* and the June 2015 issue of *Entertainment Weekly*.

Regarding the massive recognition and appreciation for her work, Cox told *The Telegraph*, "It's been incredible to have one show change your life so completely. I was just on

Laverne Cox and her mother, Gloria, stand next to Cox's wax figure at Madame Tussauds Wax Museum in San Francisco, California, on June 26, 2015.

the cover of *Variety* magazine. I won a daytime Emmy award last month. I won a SAG award. I've met the President, twice. It's insane."

During San Francisco Pride in June 2015, Cox was honored when Three Twins Ice Cream renamed its chocolate orange confetti ice cream "Laverne Cox's Chocolate *Orange Is the New Black*." That same month, she became the first openly transgender person with a wax figure at Madame Tussauds Wax Museum in San Francisco.

"Unfortunately, because of the historic moment that we're living in, it is still necessary to explain what it means to be transgender," Laverne Cox told Sam Roberts of SiriusXM's Sam Roberts' Friday Show in June 2014. She explained then that it is time to get beyond a basic conversation about what it means to be transgender. There's so much more to say about it, and Cox wants to expand the conversation and discuss the issues affecting the transgender community today. She continued:

> *I dream about a day, and I want to bring into fruition a day, when we don't have to have these conversations any more. And when trans people can walk down the street and not be called [a name], or have our lives threatened because of we are who we are. [We] won't be fired*

from a job simply for being who we are. I dream about that day, and I think the only way that that can happen is if we begin to have conversations that are difficult sometimes, or conversations that are uncomfortable...[and] hopefully we can do that with love and empathy.

With the groundbreaking work she has done both leading up to and since that interview, Cox is truly bringing about the day she once dreamed about.

TIMELINE

2003 Cox is cast in the independent film *Daughter of Arabia.*

2008 Cox is a contestant on VH1's *I Want to Work for Diddy.* She is the first African American transgender woman to participate on a reality competition show.

2010 Cox is the first African American transgender woman to produce and star in her own television show, VH1's *TRANSForm Me.*

2012 Cox plays a disabled African American transgender woman, Chantelle, in *Musical Chairs.*

2013 Cox plays Sophia Burset in the Netflix series *Orange Is the New Black.*

2014 On April 12, Cox receives the Stephen F. Kolzak Award at the 25th annual GLAAD Media Awards.

2014 Cox is featured on the June cover of *Time* magazine, making her the first openly transgender person to do so in the magazine's history.

2014 Cox receives a Primetime Emmy nomination in the Outstanding Guest Actor in a Comedy Series category. It's the first time an openly transgender actor has been nominated for a Primetime Emmy.

2014 Cox is named Woman of the Year by *Glamour* magazine.

2015 Cox wins a Daytime Creative Arts Emmy for her documentary *Laverne Cox Presents: The T Word.*

2015 Cox is featured on the May cover of *Variety* magazine and the June cover of *Entertainment Weekly.*

2015 Cox is included on *Time* magazine's "The 100 Most Influential People" list.

2015 Cox plays Deathy in *Grandma.*

2016 Cox scores the role of Dr. Frank-N-Furter in the Fox remake of *The Rocky Horror Picture Show.*

2016 Cox co-produces the documentary *FREE CeCe.*

GLOSSARY

ANDROGYNY The blending of feminine and masculine characteristics, and publicly expressing it in appearance and behavior.

ANTI-SEMITISM Discrimination against Jews as a religious, ethnic, or racial group.

COMMISSARY A prison-based store that sells food and supplies.

COUTURE The business of designing, making, or selling fashionable—and often custom-made—clothes.

CULOTTES A garment that is a both a skirt and a pair of pants.

DISCRIMINATION A prejudiced outlook, act, or treatment.

DISPARATE Made up of essentially different and often inconsistent elements.

DRAG QUEEN A male individual who, in performance, wears clothing often associated with women.

EMPATHY The act of being sensitive to and understanding others' thoughts, feelings, and experiences.

GENDER AFFIRMATION SURGERY A doctor-supervised surgical intervention that some transgender people choose to undergo as part of their transition. The details of such surgeries are generally private matters between a patient and their doctor.

GENDER IDENTITY A person's internal sense of gender, often expressed through behavior, clothing, hairstyle, voice, or body characteristics.

HOMICIDE The act of murder.

HOMOPHOBIA A fear or discrimination of homosexuals or homosexuality.

LGBTQ An acronym for "Lesbian, Gay, Bisexual, Transgender, and Queer/Questioning." Also commonly given as LGBT.

MEMOIR A written account of one's life and experiences.

MOSAIC Something made up of different things that together form a pattern.

OUTING The revelation (at times, involuntary) of an identity that was previously unknown to others.

PATRIARCH A man who control his family, an organization, or holds a high official position.

SEXISM The unfair treatment of others due to their gender identity.

TRAFFICKING The illegal movement of commercial goods or sex workers.

TRANSVESTITE A person who wears clothing typically associated with a gender other than the one with which they identify.

VIGIL An event at which people take time to quietly honor, remember, and pray.

FOR MORE INFORMATION

American Foundation for Suicide Prevention
   (AFSP)
120 Wall Street, 29th Floor
New York, NY 10005
(212) 363-3500
Website: http://www.afsp.org
AFSP fights against suicide. Its eighty chapters
   offer educational programs, advocacy in public policy, and support for those who have
   been affected by suicide.

Bullying Canada
471 Smythe Street
P.O. Box 27009
Fredericton, NB E3B 9M1
Canada
(877) 352-4497
Website: http://bullyingcanada.ca
Bullying Canada is Canada's first youth-created
   anti-bullying website and its only national
   anti-bullying charity. It offers a free, 24/7
   hotline for victims, perpetrators, bystanders,
   and allies.

Canadian Association for Suicide Prevention
   (CASP)
285 Benjamin Road
Waterloo, ON N2J 3Z4

Canada
(519) 884-1470 ext. 2277
Website: http://suicideprevention.ca
CASP strives to reduce the suicide rate by
    providing information and resources to
    Canadian communities.

GLAAD
5455 Wilshire Boulevard, #1500
Los Angeles, CA 90036
(323) 933-2240
Website: http://www.glaad.org
GLAAD works to amplify the voice of the
    LGBTQ community. Its members work for cul-
    tural change and "promotes understanding,
    increases acceptance, and advances equality."

National Center for Transgender Equality
    (NCTE)
1400 16th Street NW, Suite 510
Washington, DC 20036
(202) 642-4542
Website: http://www.transequality.org
The National Center for Transgender Equality
    (NCTE) is the country's leading social justice
    advocacy organization for transgender peo-
    ple. Founded in 2003, NCTE advocates for
    transgender issues at the local, state, and

federal levels, working to change laws, policies, and societal attitudes.

National Suicide Prevention Lifeline
(800) 273-8255
Website: http://www.suicidepreventionlifeline
.org
The National Suicide Prevention Lifeline is a network of 164 crisis centers in forty-nine states. It offers free, confidential, and 24/7 emotional support to those in crisis, no matter a person's age or identity.

TransKids Purple Rainbow Foundation (TKPRF)
Website: http://www.transkidspurplerainbow
.org
Since 2012, TKPRF has supported trans children and their families with education scholarships, special events, health care, and financial support for homeless trans youth and families. TKPRF also donates funds for research.

Trans Lifeline
San Francisco, CA
United States: (877) 565-8860
Canada: (877) 330-6366
Website: http://hotline.translifeline.org

Trans Lifeline offers a hotline that is "staffed by transgender people for transgender people." Its culturally competent service is free and confidential, empowering those going through the "darkest moments of their lives," namely gender identity struggles and suicide.

Trans Youth Equality Foundation (TYEF)
P.O. Box 7441
Portland, ME 04112
(207) 478-4087
Website: http://www.transyouthequality.org
TYEF offers support, advocacy, and education for transgender and gender non-conforming youth and their families.

TransYouth Family Allies (TYFA)
P.O. Box 1471
Holland, MI 49422
(888) 462-8932
Website: http://www.imatyfa.org
TYFA helps trans children and families by partnering with educators, service providers, and communities to develop supportive environments in which gender may be expressed and respected.

The Trevor Project
P.O. Box 69232
West Hollywood, CA 90069
(866) 488-7386
Website: http://www.thetrevorproject.org
In 1998, the creators of the Academy Award–
  winning short film *TREVOR*, formed The
  Trevor Project. This national organization
  offers crisis intervention and suicide prevention services to lesbian, gay, bisexual,
  transgender, and questioning (LGBTQ)
  people ages twenty-four and younger.

WEBSITES

Because of the changing nature of Internet
links, Rosen Publishing has developed an
online list of websites related to the subject of
this book. This site is updated regularly. Please
use this link to access the list:

http://www.rosenlinks.com/TGP/cox

FOR FURTHER READING

Belge, Kathy, and Marke Bieschke. *Queer: The Ultimate LGBT Guide for Teens*. San Francisco, CA: Zest Books, 2011.

Boedecker, Anne L. *The Transgender Guidebook: Keys to a Successful Transition*. North Charleston, SC: CreateSpace Independent Publishing Platform, 2011.

Boylan, Jennifer Finney. *She's Not There: A Life in Two Genders*. New York, NY: Broadway Paperbacks, 2013.

Boylan, Jennifer Finney. *Stuck in the Middle with You: A Memoir of Parenting in Three Genders*. New York, NY: Broadway Books, 2013.

Duron, Lori. *Raising My Rainbow: Adventures in Raising a Fabulous, Gender Creative Son*. New York, NY: Broadway Books, 2013.

Ehrensaft, Diane. *Gender Born, Gender Made: Raising Healthy Gender-Nonconforming Children*. New York, NY: The Experiment, LLC, 2011.

Erickson-Schroth, Laura, ed. *Trans Bodies, Trans Selves: A Resource for the Transgender Community*. New York, NY: Oxford University Press, 2014.

Herthel, Jessica, and Jazz Jennings. *I Am Jazz*. New York, NY: Dial Books For Young Readers, 2014.

Hubbard, Dr. Eleanor A., and Cameron T. Whitley, eds. *Trans-Kin: A Guide for Family and Friends of Transgender People*. Volume 1. Boulder, CO: Boulder Press, 2012.

Huegel, Kelly. *GLBTQ: The Survival Guide for Gay, Lesbian, Bisexual, Transgender, and Questioning Teens*. Minneapolis, MN: Free Spirit Publishing Inc., 2011.

Kerman, Piper. *Orange Is the New Black: My Year in a Women's Prison*. New York, NY: Spiegel & Grau, 2010.

Krieger, Irwin. *Helping Your Transgender Teen: A Guide for Parents*. New Haven, CT: Genderwise Press, 2011.

Kuklin, Susan. *Beyond Magenta: Transgender Teens Speak Out*. Somerville, MA: Candlewick Press, 2014.

Manske, Nathan, ed. *I'm from Driftwood: Lesbian, Gay, Bisexual, Transgender & Queer Stories from All Over the World*. Portland, OR: BookBaby, 2010.

Mock, Janet. *Redefining Realness: My Path to Womanhood, Identity, Love & So Much More*. New York, NY: Atria Books, 2014.

Nutt, Amy Ellis. *Becoming Nicole: The Transformation of an American Family*. New York, NY: Random House, 2015.

Pepper, Rachel. *Transitions of the Heart: Stories of Love, Struggle and Acceptance by Mothers of Transgender and Gender Variant Children.* Berkeley, CA: Cleis Press Inc., 2012.

Savage, Dan, and Terry Miller, ed. *It Gets Better: Coming Out, Overcoming Bullying, and Creating a Life Worth Living.* New York, NY: Penguin Group (USA) Inc., 2012.

Teich, Nicholas M. *Transgender 101: A Simple Guide to a Complex Issue.* New York, NY: Columbia University Press, 2012.

Testa, Rylan Jay, Deborah Coolhart, Jayme Peta, and Arlene Istar Lev. *The Gender Quest Workbook: A Guide for Teens and Young Adults Exploring Gender Identity.* Oakland, CA: Instant Help Books, 2015.

Waldron, Candace. *My Daughter He: Transitioning with Our Transgender Children.* Rockport, MA: Stone Circle Press, 2014.

BIBLIOGRAPHY

Allen, Samantha. "The Trans Murder That Started a Movement." TheDailyBeast.com. Retrieved November 23, 2015 (http://www.thedailybeast.com).

ASFA Aspiring Minds. "Laverne Cox." Inspiring Stories. ASFA. Retrieved October 21, 2015 (http://www.asfa.k12.al.us/apps/pages/index.jsp?uREC_ID=280016&type=d).

Benincasa, Sara. "Laverne Cox Spills On Self-Acceptance, Finding Love & Battling The Patriachy (BUST Exclusive)." Bust.com. Retrieved November 8, 2015 (http://bust.com).

Bigham, Gina. Interview by Erin Staley. Riverside, CA: November 1, 2014.

Bissinger, Buzz. "Caitlyn Jenner: The Full Story." VanityFair.com. Retrieved November 26, 2015 (http://www.vanityfair.com).

Borrego, Dee. "Who Was Rita Hester?" 50.50 inclusive democracy. Retrieved November 23, 2015 (https://www.opendemocracy.net/5050/dee-borrego/who-was-rita-hester).

Breen, Matthew. "Laverne Cox: The Making of an Icon." Advocate.com. Retrieved October 17, 2015 (http://www.advocate.com).

Coleman, Miriam. "Jennifer Lopez, Laverne Cox Honored at GLAAD Media Awards." RollingStone.com. Retrieved November 11,

2015 (http://www.rollingstone.com).

Colurso, Mary. "Alabama's Laverne Cox Hosts #GoBOLD Video Series, Part of Revlon Ad Campaign in Cosmopolitan." AL.com. Retrieved November 28, 2015 (http://www.al.com).

CornelWest.com. "About Dr. Cornel West." Retrieved November 21, 2015 (http://www.cornelwest.com/bio.html#.VlD3F3arTlU).

Cox, Laverne. Official Laverne Cox Tumblr. Retrieved November 30, 2015 (http://lavernecox.tumblr.com).

Cox, Laverne. "Singer Sir Ari Gold Talks About His Childhood and Being a Sex Symbol, and He Goes 3D for His Latest Video." Huff Post Gay Voices. Retrieved October 8, 2015 (http://www.huffingtonpost.com/laverne-cox/sir-ari-gold_b_3520468.html).

Cox, Laverne. "Why My New Film, Musical Chairs, Is a Career Milestone for Me." HuffPost Gay Voices. Retrieved November 28, 2015 (http://www.huffingtonpost.com/laverne-cox/musical-chairs-film_b_1374329.html).

Delbyck, Cole. "Laverne Cox Takes Lead Role In 'Rocky Horror' TV Remake." HuffingtonPost.com. Retrieved November 14, 2015 (http://www.huffingtonpost.com).

GLAAD.org. "GLAAD Media Reference Guide

- Transgender Issues." Retrieved October 21, 2015 (http://www.glaad.org/reference/transgender).

GLAAD.org. "Jennifer Lopez, Laverne Cox Honored at 25th Annual GLAAD Media Awards." Retrieved November 30, 2015 (http://www.glaad.org).

Grant, Jaime M., Lisa A. Mottet, Justin Tanis, Jack Harrison, Jody L. Herman, and Mara Keisling. "Injustice at Every Turn: A Report of the National Transgender Discrimination Survey." National Center for Transgender Equality and National Gay and Lesbian Task Force. 2011. Retrieved October 19, 2015 (http://www.transequality.org/sites/default/files/docs/resources/NTDS_Report.pdf).

Haas, Ann P., Philip L. Rodgers, and Jody L. Herman. "Suicide Attempts Among Transgender and Gender Non-Conforming Adults: Findings of the National Transgender Discrimination Survey." Retrieved November 25, 2015 (http://williamsinstitute.law.ucla.edu).

Kang, Andy. "Laverne Cox Educates Hosts on 'CBS This Morning' and Talks About Her Success on Orange Is the New Black." GLAAD.org. Retrieved November 26, 2015 (http://www.glaad.org).

LaverneCox.com. "Laverne Cox." Retrieved

November 24, 2015 (http://www.lavernecox
.com/bio-2).

Matthews, Michelle. "Laverne Cox's Time Has
Come, and Her Mother in Mobile Is Her No.
1 Fan." AL.com. Retrieved October 18, 2015
(http://www.al.com).

Mulkerrins, Jane. "Laverne Cox: On Growing Up
Trans, Orange Is the New Black and Caitlyn
Jenner." Telegraph.com. Retrieved October 8,
2015 (http://www.telegraph.co.uk).

Nichols, James Michael. "Laverne Cox to Produce 'Trans Teen: The Documentary' With MTV
And Logo." HuffingtonPost.com. Retrieved
November 26, 2015 (http://www
.huffingtonpost.com).

Nicholson, Rebecca. "Laverne Cox: 'Now I Have
the Money to Feminise My Face I Don't Want
To. I'm happy That This Is the Face God Gave
Me.'" TheGuardian.com. Retrieved November
11, 2015 (http://www.theguardian.com).

NPR.org. "'Orange' Creator Jenji Kohan: 'Piper
Was My Trojan Horse.'" Retrieved November
21, 2015 (http://www.npr.org).

PiperKerman.com. "Piper Kerman." Retrieved
November 11, 2015 (http://piperkerman.com/).

Ring, Trudy. "Laverne Cox Gets Ice Cream
Flavor Named for Her for Pride." Advocate

.com. Retrieved November 30, 2015 (http://
www.advocate.com).

Sandberg, Bryn Elise. "'Orange Is the New Black'
Casting Director Reveals How She Found
Diverse Stars." HollywoodReporter.com.
Retrieved November 21, 2015 (http://www
.hollywoodreporter.com/news/orange-is
-new-black-casting-723404).

Signorile, Michelangelo. "Laverne Cox Talks
Performing In Nightclubs, 'Orange Is The
New Black' and More." Huffpost Gay Voices.
Retrieved November 11, 2015 (http://www
.huffingtonpost.com).

Smith, Gwendolyn Ann. "Transgender Day of
Remembrance: Rita Hester and Beyond." Huff-
ingtonPost.com. Retrieved November 23, 2015
(http://www.huffingtonpost.com/).

Steinmetz, Katy. "Laverne Cox Talks to TIME
About the Transgender Movement." TIME.
com. Retrieved October 14, 2015 (http://time.
com/132769/transgender-orange-is-the-new
-black-laverne-cox-interview/).

VH1.com. "I Want to Work for Diddy." Retrieved
November 25, 2015 (http://www.vh1.com
/shows/i_want_to_work_for_diddy/).

YouTube. "It Got Better Featuring Laverne Cox
| L/Studio created by Lexus." June 11, 2014

(https://www.youtube.com/watch?v=
1MfxtM9N3fw).

YouTube. "Laverne Cox Ain't I a Woman: My
Journey to Womanhood + Q&A!" October 24, 2014 (https://www.youtube.com/
watch?v=iKOVXsMbvWQ).

YouTube. "Laverne Cox Opens Up About 'TIME'
Cover & 'Orange is the New Black'." June 10,
2014 (https://www.youtube.com/watch?v=
3mgBwCxTRDY).

YouTube. "Laverne Cox - Working for Diddy,
Transphobia, & Orange." June18, 2014
(https://www.youtube.com/watch?v=
dB36i4ePgAQ).

YouTube. "Orange Is The New Black Season 2
Cast Interview Laverne Cox SUBTITULADO."
May 8, 2014 (https://www.youtube.com/
watch?v=_sxA-w0fGrw).

YouTube. "'Orange Is the New Black' Star
Laverne Cox." June 9, 2014 (https://www
.youtube.com/watch?v=FuZIp26WUKE).

YouTube. "Sam Roberts & Laverne Cox - Orange,
Diddy, Being Trans, Language, etc." June 14,
2014 (https://www.youtube.com/watch?v=B
-QRT79QYXQ).

YouTube. "The Story Of Jazz." January 19, 2013
(https://www.youtube.com/watch?v=Xt_wLU
_EB2w).

INDEX

ABOUT THE AUTHOR

After running a successful dance program for over a decade, Erin Staley took her stories from the stage to the page as an author. Forever a student of the human condition, Erin fostered a passion for history, technology, and the enduring spirit of pioneers in their fields of interest. Today, she writes for the University of California, Riverside, as an international recruitment creative copywriter.

PHOTO CREDITS

Cover, p. 1 Rabbani and Solimene Photography/WireImage/Getty Images; pp. 4–5 Tommaso Boddi/WireImage/Getty Images; p. 10 Gabriel Olsen/Getty Images; p. 11 Ozan Kose/AFP/Getty Images; p. 15 Frederick M. Brown/Getty Images; pp. 24, 35 Helga Esteb/Shutterstock.com; p. 27 Wasted Time R/Wikimedia/File:MarymountManhattanCollege.jpg/CC BY-SA 3.0; p. 30 Courtesy Everett Collection; p. 37 John Parra/Getty Images; p. 40 © Roadside Attractions/courtesy Everett Collection; p. 44 Jim Spellman/WireImage/Getty Images; p. 47 Sonia Recchia/Getty Images; p. 50 Debby Wong/Shutterstock.com; p. 52 Jamie McCarthy/Getty Images; p. 54 Eric Leibowitz/ © Netflix/courtesy Everett Collection; p. 57 JoJo Whilden/ © Netflix/courtesy Everett Collection; p. 62 © epa european pressphoto agency b.v./Alamy Stock Photo; p. 68 Hulton Archive/Getty Images; p. 70 David Surowiecki/Getty Images; p. 72 Jason Kempin/Getty Images; p. 75 Larry Busacca/Getty Images; p. 80 © Jerry Holt/Minneapolis Star Tribune/ZUMA Press: p. 83 Rahav Segev/FilmMagic/Getty Images; pp. 86–87 Mike Coppola/Getty Images; pp. 88–89 Arun Nevader/Getty Images; cover and interior pages graphic pattern L. Kramer/Shutterstock.com.
Designer: Ellina Litmanovich; Photo Researcher: Carina Finn